DAY TO DAY

Easy recipes for everyday cooking and instant entertaining

For my husband and family,
who love good eating

Phillippa Cheifitz

DAY TO DAY

Easy recipes for everyday cooking and instant entertaining

CONTENTS

INTRODUCTION

This is the cookbook to keep in the kitchen to use everyday. It's a blueprint of easy, fabulous recipes that will please the family and impress friends. Simple-to-follow instructions promise perfect fast-roast chicken, a great steak, the ultimate Caesar salad. With all the twists and variations on the basic recipe, here is an extensive repertoire that will make daily cooking interesting, never monotonous, and always a pleasure. What fun to enjoy cooking and eating well, whether preparing for four or more, just for the two of you, or spoiling yourself.

ONE SIMPLE BROTH,
Four super soups

Take one basic chicken broth,
then flavour it four ways to create four deliciously different soups.

BASIC CHICKEN BROTH

I use chicken wings as all the bones give the broth gelatinous strength. (And I love the cooked chicken wings Asian-style, with soy sauce, sesame oil, chopped ginger and spring onions.)

2 packs free-range chicken wings (about 16)
8–10 cups water
1 large onion, halved
1 bunch celery, roughly cut
handful of parsley
6 carrots, scrubbed and split
1 bay leaf
2 teaspoons salt
½ teaspoon peppercorns

Wash the wings well and place in a saucepan with the water. Slowly bring to the boil, skim the surface, then add the rest of the ingredients. Cover (almost) and reduce the heat so that the broth gently simmers for about 2 hours. Strain, cool and chill. Spoon off the layer of fat before reheating. Check seasoning. **MAKES 6 CUPS**

Moroccan-style soup

6 cups basic chicken broth (page 9)
pinch of saffron
1 cinnamon stick
1 red chilli, seeded and chopped
1 x 400 g tin chopped tomatoes
1 x 400 g tin chickpeas, drained and rinsed
2–3 baby marrows, thinly sliced
1–2 carrots, thinly sliced
handful of chopped coriander leaves
couscous
harissa paste (chilli-based paste, available from good food stores)

Simmer the broth with the saffron, cinnamon, chilli, tomatoes, chickpeas, baby marrows and carrots for about 15 minutes. Discard the cinnamon and stir in the coriander. Serve over scoops of hot couscous with harissa paste on the side. **SERVES 4–6**

Jewish-style soup

6 cups basic chicken broth (page 9)
4 nests of lokshen (fine vermicelli)
salt and ground pepper
finely chopped parsley

MATZO DUMPLINGS:
2 free-range eggs
2 tablespoons sunflower oil
2 tablespoons basic chicken broth
½ cup matzo meal
½ teaspoon baking powder
salt and white pepper

Make the dumplings first. Beat the eggs with the oil and broth. Stir in the matzo meal, baking powder (unorthodox, but it facilitates fluffiness) and seasoning to taste. With wet hands, form into eight balls (think golf balls). Simmer in a large saucepan of salted boiling water, covered, for 20 minutes, or until puffed and cooked through.

To make the soup, simmer the broth with the noodles until tender. Check seasoning. Sprinkle with parsley and serve with hot matzo dumplings. SERVES 4–6

Mexican-style soup

6 cups basic chicken broth (page 9)
1 punnet baby corn (about 125 g)
handful of coriander leaves
1 green chilli, chopped
1 firm ripe avocado, diced
1–2 unpeeled limes, sliced
salt and ground pepper
strips of flour tortilla, crisply fried

Heat the broth with the corn. Stir in the coriander, chilli, avocado and limes. Check seasoning. Serve immediately, topped with golden, crisp tortilla strips. **SERVES 4–6**

Greek-style soup

6 cups basic chicken broth (page 9)
½ cup rice
2 free-range eggs
juice of 2 lemons
handful of baby spinach, shredded
2 tablespoons chopped dill
salt and ground pepper

Heat the broth with the rice, covered, and cook for about 15 minutes, or until the rice is tender. In a bowl, whisk the eggs. Gradually whisk in the strained lemon juice until frothy, then whisk this mixture into the soup until heated through. Stir in the spinach and dill and check seasoning. Serve immediately.
SERVES 4–6

ONE EASY SOUP,
Five ways to savour

Take this simple vegetable soup
from family supper to dinner for friends.

BASIC COUNTRY SOUP

2–3 tablespoons butter/sunflower oil
1 bunch leeks (about 250 g), washed and sliced
2–3 potatoes (about 450 g), peeled and chopped
3 cups chicken/vegetable stock
salt and white pepper
chives for garnishing

Heat the butter/oil, add the sliced leeks (mainly the white part) and a pinch of salt. Cook very gently until soft but still pale. Add the potatoes and toss around with the leeks. Pour in the stock and bring to a bubble, reduce the heat and half cover. Simmer for about 20 minutes, or until the vegetables are soft. Blend with a hand-held blender, not too smoothly, so that it has a chunky texture. If necessary, thin down with more stock or full-cream milk. Sprinkle with snipped chives.

Serve with crusty croutons (page 22); grated gruyère cheese; crumbled crispy bacon; or deep-fried shredded leek. **SERVES 4**

Vichyssoise

To turn the basic country soup (above) into an elegant cold one, blend until very smooth. If it's too thick, thin it down with extra stock. Enrich with ½ cup cream and chill well. (For a less rich alternative, use buttermilk instead of cream.)

Serve with a sprinkling of snipped chives and chive flowers, if available. **SERVES 4**

Butternut soup

Add 500 g cubed butternut and 1 crushed clove garlic to the basic country soup (page 17). Serve with small cheese toasts (page 22); or with freshly grated Parmesan cheese and finely chopped parsley. **SERVES 4–6**

Fennel & salmon soup

Use 1–2 bulbs fennel instead of leeks in the basic country soup recipe (page 17). Switch off the heat and add chunks of fresh salmon trout (about 200 g). Cover and leave to cook. Thin down with extra stock if necessary, or enrich with ¼–⅓ cup cream. Leave the soup chunky. Serve with chopped fennel fronds and a dollop of thick mayonnaise. **SERVES 4–6**

Creamy watercress soup

Follow the basic country soup recipe (page 17), then remove from the stove and stir in about 100 g washed watercress. The heat will wilt the cress, but it should stay a bright colour. Blend until smooth, then thin down, if necessary, with extra stock. Swirl in ⅓ cup cream.

Serve with sprigs of watercress to garnish. **SERVES 4–6**

Dill mushroom soup

Add 250 g sliced button mushrooms to the basic country soup (page 17), and a handful of chopped dill with the potatoes. If necessary, thin it down with extra stock.

Serve with a dollop of thick sour cream, chopped dill and a sprinkling of paprika; or add fried, sliced mushrooms and paprika. **SERVES 4–6**

SOUP ESSENTIALS

TRADITIONAL CROUTONS
Lightly toast slices of day-old bread (white or wholewheat) and trim the crusts. Cut into neat, small cubes and fry in a mixture of hot oil and butter (or only oil), not too many at a time, stirring very often until golden brown. Add more oil as needed. Drain croutons well on paper towels.

OVEN-BAKED CROUTONS
Tear irregular pieces of bread and sprinkle with grated Parmesan cheese. Toast in the oven at 190 °C, turning once, for about 15 minutes, or until crisp and golden.

CHEESE TOASTS
Slice panini (or a very slim baguette). Brush the slices with olive oil and lightly toast under the grill. Top with grated gruyère cheese, shavings of Parmesan or slices of soft goat cheese. Slide under the grill again until melted and golden.

ONE CLASSIC SALAD,
Four terrific twists

The better and fresher the ingredients,
the greater the salad.

CLASSIC CAESAR SALAD

3–4 cos lettuces
about 75 g Parmesan cheese, freshly grated

GARLIC CROUTONS:
½ loaf day-old ciabatta/country-style bread
about ½ cup olive oil
1–2 cloves garlic, crushed
salt and ground pepper

DRESSING:
1 free-range egg
1 tablespoon red wine vinegar
3 tablespoons freshly squeezed lemon juice
2 teaspoons Dijon mustard
1 clove garlic, crushed
about 6 anchovy fillets, rinsed, dried,
chopped and smashed
salt and ground pepper
⅔ cup olive oil
handful of freshly grated Parmesan cheese

FOR THE GARLIC CROUTONS:
Break off pieces of bread. Gently heat the olive oil with the garlic in a roasting pan at 180 °C until aromatic. Toss the bread in the garlic oil, then flatten into a single layer and bake for about 10 minutes, or until golden and crisp, tossing halfway through. Season lightly.

FOR THE DRESSING:
Blend the egg with the vinegar, lemon juice, mustard, garlic, anchovies, a little salt and lots of black pepper. Blend or whisk in the oil. Stir in the Parmesan and check seasoning.

TO SERVE THE SALAD:
Discard the outer lettuce leaves. Cut off the base of each lettuce and separate into leaves. Wash and dry the leaves well, leaving them whole. Place in a large bowl. Add most of the dressing and toss. Add the croutons and most of the cheese and toss again.

Serve in one large bowl, on a platter, or divide among four bowls or plates. Add the rest of the Parmesan, moisten with the remaining dressing and grind over a twist or two of black pepper. **SERVES 4**

... with pan-grilled chicken breast

4 skinless free-range chicken fillets (about 100 g each)
salt and ground pepper
olive oil

Season the chicken portions and moisten with oil. Place in a cold, ungreased non-stick pan. Turn on the heat to medium and cook until golden and the flesh still moist. Flip to lightly brown the other side.

Allow to cool to room temperature. Slice across and mix with about one-third of the salad dressing. Add to the salad along with the croutons. **SERVES 4**

... with roast diced potatoes

500 g potatoes, scrubbed but unpeeled
salt and ground pepper
olive oil

Cut the potatoes into cubes, season and moisten with oil. Arrange in a single layer in an oiled roasting pan and roast at 230 °C, one shelf above the middle of the oven, for about 30 minutes until crisp, golden and tender. Turn over about three-quarter way through the cooking time. Add to the salad instead of the croutons. **SERVES 4**

... with seared tuna

1 thick tuna steak (400–500 g)
salt and ground pepper
olive oil

Season the tuna and moisten with oil. Heat a ridged, cast-iron pan, coated with a non-stick cooking spray, and when it's really hot, add the tuna. Sear on both sides so that it is very rare inside.

Allow to cool to room temperature. Separate into chunks and mix with about one-third of the salad dressing. Add to the salad along with the croutons. **SERVES 4**

... with avocado & biltong

1–2 firm, ripe avocados
about 80 g crispy biltong

Slice the avocado and mix with about one-third of the dressing.
Gently toss the avo with the mixed salad. Shred the biltong and
add to the salad along with the croutons. **SERVES 4**

ONE SIMPLE SAUCE,
Four fabulous pastas

Master one classic sauce (good enough as is),
then use it for four impressively easy pasta dishes.

BASIC TOMATO PASTA SAUCE

¼ cup olive oil
1 onion, finely chopped
1 stick celery, finely chopped
salt and ground pepper
1–2 cloves garlic, chopped
2 x 400 g tins whole, peeled tomatoes in juice
1 x 70 g tin tomato paste
2 tablespoons chopped parsley
1 teaspoon dried oregano
1 small bay leaf

FOR SERVING:
500 g spaghetti
freshly grated Parmesan cheese
olive oil for drizzling
chopped Italian parsley or shredded basil leaves

Pour the oil into a suitable saucepan. Add the onion and celery. Cook gently, with a little salt and pepper, until very soft but not browned. Stir in the garlic, then the tomatoes. Crush in the pan using a potato masher. Add the tomato paste, herbs and some more seasoning. Simmer very gently, uncovered, stirring now and again, for about 45 minutes, or until reduced and thickened. Discard the bay leaf and check seasoning. If it seems too acidic, stir in a pinch of sugar.

Serve as is for a rough, robust texture or purée with a hand-held blender for a smooth sauce. Toss just-cooked spaghetti with half the sauce, then pass around the rest. Sprinkle with Parmesan and drizzle with the best olive oil. Sprinkle with parsley or basil leaves. **MAKES 2 CUPS**

Fusilli with roasted corn & pumpkin

4 corn on the cob
500 g peeled, diced pumpkin
olive oil
salt and ground pepper

FOR SERVING:
500 g fusilli (or any spiral pasta)
2 cups chunky basic tomato pasta sauce (page 33)
deep-fried sage leaves
grated goat pecorino cheese

With a sharp knife, slice the corn kernels off the cob. Turn onto a baking sheet. Add the diced pumpkin. Mix together and moisten with oil and seasoning. Flatten into a single layer. Roast at 230 °C one rack above the middle of the oven, for about 30 minutes, or until tender and starting to char.

Toss the just-cooked pasta with the basic tomato pasta sauce and top with the roasted vegetables and deep-fried sage. Pass around grated pecorino cheese. **SERVES 6**

Spaghettini with broccoli & anchovy

½ cup olive oil
50 g anchovy fillets, chopped
2–3 cloves garlic, chopped
1 fresh chilli, chopped (optional)
400 g broccoli florets, blanched
salt and ground pepper

FOR SERVING:
400 g spaghettini
2 cups smooth basic tomato
   pasta sauce (page 33)
freshly grated Parmesan cheese

Heat the oil with the anchovies, garlic
and chilli (if using), stirring until the
anchovies disintegrate. Stir in the
broccoli and cook until very tender.
Check seasoning.

   Mix together with the just-cooked
pasta. Serve the basic tomato pasta
sauce on the side and sprinkle
generously with Parmesan.
SERVES 4–6

Penne with spicy sausage sauce

2 cups chunky basic tomato
   pasta sauce (cooked with 1 split
   red chilli) (page 33)
about 250 g chorizo sausage, sliced
handful of coriander leaves
salt and ground pepper

FOR SERVING:
440 g penne
about 125 g feta cheese
olive oil for drizzling

Cook the basic tomato pasta sauce
with a split chilli. Pan-fry sliced chorizo
(you shouldn't need oil) and mix with
the hot tomato sauce. Add fresh
coriander leaves. Check seasoning.

   Toss the just-cooked pasta with the
sauce. Sprinkle with crumbled feta and
drizzle with olive oil. SERVES 4–6

Linguine with seafood sauce

1 cup cream
1 fat clove garlic, crushed
250 g seafood mix, at room temperature, rinsed
   and drained
handful of shredded basil leaves
salt and ground pepper

FOR SERVING:
400 g linguine
2 cups smooth basic tomato pasta sauce (page 33)
basil leaves

Simmer the cream with the garlic until slightly reduced and slightly thickened. Add the seafood and cook for barely a minute until just cooked. Stir in basil and seasoning to taste. Toss the hot basic tomato pasta sauce with just-cooked pasta, spoon over the seafood sauce and garnish with basil leaves. **SERVES 4–6**

ONE BASIC RISOTTO,
Four stirring flavours

Once you know how easy it is to prepare,
you'll make it as often as pasta.

BASIC RISOTTO

3 tablespoons unsalted butter or olive oil (or a mix of both)
1 onion, chopped
1 clove garlic, crushed
1½ cups risotto rice
about 4 cups hot chicken or vegetable stock (or a mix of both)
½ cup dry white wine or extra-dry vermouth
a few tablespoons chopped Italian parsley
about 1 cup freshly grated Parmesan cheese
salt and ground pepper
2–3 tablespoons butter, cut into pieces

Heat the butter/oil in a large, wide and heavy saucepan and gently fry the onion with a pinch of salt until soft but not browned. Add the garlic and rice, stirring constantly, until well coated. Pour in a few ladles of hot stock and stir until the rice has absorbed the liquid. Repeat, adding the wine/vermouth towards the end, until the rice is tender, swollen and creamy (not soggy, chewy or gritty). Stir in parsley and half the Parmesan.

Check seasoning – it may not need salt but add a grinding of pepper. Add the bits of butter, cover tightly and leave for a few minutes, then serve immediately, sprinkled with the rest of the Parmesan. Great with braised veal knuckles. **SERVES 4–6 (STARTER), 8 AS A SIDE DISH**

THE PERFECT RISOTTO

- Preparation time for a risotto is approximately 25 minutes.
- Choose the correct rice, Arborio or Carnaroli, to get the right texture.
- Use a wide, heavy-bottomed pan or casserole dish that distributes heat evenly.

Mixed pea risotto

Follow the basic risotto recipe (page 41), but before adding the stock use it to blanch 100 g each of frozen peas, trimmed mangetouts and trimmed sugarsnap peas. When the rice is almost ready, add ¼–⅓ cup warm cream (instead of butter bits) and the blanched peas and allow to heat through. Check seasoning and sprinkle generously with grated Parmesan.

Great with roast lamb, in which case omit the Parmesan and add a sprinkling of chopped fresh mint. **SERVES 4–6 (STARTER), 8 AS A SIDE DISH**

Pumpkin & sage risotto

Follow the basic risotto recipe (page 41), using olive oil only and double the garlic. Add a spoonful or two of torn fresh sage to the stock. When the rice is almost ready, stir in 500 g roasted pumpkin chunks (at room temperature) with the last ladles of broth.

Check seasoning. Crisply fry a handful of sage leaves in butter, then spoon over the risotto and serve immediately, topped with shavings of Parmesan. Great with roast chicken. **SERVES 4–6 (STARTER), 8 AS A SIDE DISH**

Mushroom risotto

First stir-fry 250 g sliced fresh porcini or portabellini mushrooms in a mix of unsalted butter and olive oil – about 1 tablespoon of each. Remove and set them aside.

Soak a 20 g sachet of dried porcini mushrooms in 1 cup of hot water for about 20 minutes. Strain and use the mushroom-soaked water as part of the stock. Use a mushroom stock cube (or chicken or vegetable stock) to make up the rest of the liquid. Following the basic recipe, chop the soaked mushrooms and add them to the stock and rice. Add the fried mushrooms towards the end and heat through. Check seasoning and sprinkle with snipped chives.

You could add Parmesan, but you may prefer it without. The luxury of a drizzle of truffle oil at the table would add an extra dimension. Great with seared salmon. **SERVES 4–6 (STARTER), 8 AS A SIDE DISH**

Simple seafood risotto

You could turn it into a more serious dish, with large prawns, fresh mussels or even crayfish. But here a sachet of good quality seafood mix results in a suitable everyday dish. If you prefer, enrich it with a few spoonfuls of cream, or add a good squeeze of lemon juice.

Follow the basic risotto recipe (page 41), using olive oil only. Replace the onion with 1–2 bulbs fennel or 2–3 leeks and use a light fish stock instead of chicken or veg stock. When the rice is almost done, add 250 g seafood mix with the last ladles of stock. Cover and steam until cooked. Check seasoning. Omit butter and Parmesan and sprinkle with fennel fronds or chopped dill.

Great as a main course for two or three, with a salad of greens on the side. **SERVES 4–6**

ONE SIMPLE ROAST,
Four great chicken dishes

**Learn to fast-roast
a butterflied chicken,**
plus four delicious ways
to vary it.

FAST ROAST CHICKEN

1 free-range chicken (about 1.5 kg)
olive oil
salt and ground pepper
1 onion, thinly sliced
1 lemon, thinly sliced (optional)
2–3 cloves garlic, smashed
handful of Italian parsley, roughly chopped
handful of celery leaves, roughly chopped
1 bay leaf
1 cup chicken stock

Using strong kitchen scissors, cut out the chicken backbone (you can freeze this for broth). Wash, clean and pat the chicken dry. Moisten with olive oil and season.

Place, opened as flat as possible, on a bed of onion, lemon, garlic, parsley, celery and bay leaves in a well-oiled roasting pan. Roast uncovered at 230 °C, one shelf above the centre of the oven, for 45 minutes, or until golden brown and crisp.

Take out the chicken and keep warm. Pour the stock into the roasting pan and return to the oven for about 10 minutes.

Cut the chicken into quarters and serve immediately with the strained pan juices and whichever potatoes you fancy – roast potato wedges or baked potatoes can be conveniently cooked at the same time as the chicken, or serve with garlicky mashed potatoes. Dress a mixed leaf salad simply – a grinding of salt and pepper, a light moistening of good olive oil and a squeeze of lemon juice. Eat the potatoes and salad on the same plate as the chicken so they soak up the delicious pan juices. **SERVES 4**

Spicy roast chicken

1 free-range chicken (prepared for roasting, page 49)
3–4 tablespoons ready-made tandoori paste
sunflower oil
2 onions, very thinly sliced
1 cup chicken stock
coriander leaves for garnishing

FOR SERVING:
steamed basmati rice, mango chutney, lime pickles, thick plain
yoghurt mixed with crushed dried mint, shredded crisp lettuce

Carefully lift the skin of the prepared chicken with your hands
and rub the flesh with the tandoori paste. Moisten the skin with
sunflower oil. Place on a layer of onion in a well-oiled roasting
pan. Roast, uncovered, at 230 °C, one shelf above the centre of
the oven, for 45 minutes, or until golden brown and crisp. Remove
chicken and add the stock to the roasting pan. Cook, stirring, on
top of the stove until slightly reduced. Garnish with coriander
and serve as suggested. **SERVES 4**

Roast chicken with feta & orzo

1 free-range chicken (prepared for roasting, page 49)
about 200 g feta cheese
olive oil
4–6 cloves garlic
dried oregano
400 g orzo (rice-shaped pasta), cooked
1 x 400 g tin whole, peeled tomatoes in juice, crushed
salt and ground pepper

Crumble the feta and moisten with olive oil. Add 2–3 crushed cloves garlic, about ½ teaspoon dried oregano and a grinding of black pepper. It should be salty enough.

Carefully lift the chicken skin with your hands to loosen, then push in the feta mixture to cover the flesh.

Mix the orzo with the tomatoes, about 1 teaspoon dried oregano, 2–3 crushed cloves garlic, a little olive oil and seasoning to taste.

Turn into a well-oiled roasting pan and place the chicken on top. Roast uncovered at 230 °C, one shelf above the centre of the oven, for 45 minutes, or until golden brown and crisp. **SERVES 4**

Roast chicken & vegetables

1 free-range chicken (prepared for
roasting, page 49)
1 kg mix of whole, roasting baby vegetables
olive oil
salt and ground pepper
2 cloves garlic, thinly sliced
handful of thyme
watercress for garnishing

Place the washed and dried vegetables in a well-oiled roasting pan. Moisten lightly with oil and season. Add garlic and thyme and place the prepared chicken on top.

Roast, uncovered, at 230 °C, one shelf above the centre of the oven, for 45 minutes, or until golden brown and crisp. Garnish lavishly with watercress to serve. **SERVES 4**

Roast chicken with polenta

1 free-range chicken (prepared for
roasting, page 49)
3–4 cups cooked instant polenta
2–3 cloves garlic, crushed
handful of sage leaves
olive oil

Serve with wilted spinach, dressed simply with
olive oil, a squeeze of lemon juice and a
grinding of salt and pepper. **SERVES 4**

Spread a layer of cooked polenta in a well-oiled
roasting pan. Add the garlic and sage leaves
and moisten with olive oil. Place the prepared
chicken on top and roast, uncovered, at 230 °C,
one shelf above the centre of the oven, for
45 minutes, or until golden brown and crisp.

ONE CHICKEN FILLET,
Four ultra-healthy ways

A pan-seared chicken fillet, moist and flavoursome,
is the star of this lean cuisine.

BASIC PAN-SEARED CHICKEN FILLET

4 skinless free-range chicken fillets (500 g)
oil (olive, sunflower or peanut)
salt and ground pepper

Moisten the chicken with oil. Place in a cold, dry, non-stick pan. Turn the heat to medium-hot. Once nicely browned, flip and cook the other side until brown and the chicken is just cooked and still moist. Season to taste. Wrap in foil to keep warm and allow to rest for 5 minutes. **SERVES 4**

... with stir-fried greens

2 tablespoons peanut oil
1 clove garlic, chopped
1 chunk ginger, peeled and chopped
2–4 spring onions, finely chopped
400 g chopped Asian greens (any mix of bok choy, tatsoi, tenderstem broccoli, etc.)
1 tablespoon soy sauce
2 tablespoons sesame oil

Heat the oil in a wide, non-stick pan. Stir in the garlic and ginger, then add the spring onions and greens. Stir-fry over high heat until wilted and tender-crisp. Add the pan-seared chicken fillets (thinly sliced), soy sauce and sesame oil. Check seasoning. Add more soy or a little salt if necessary.
    Serve on steamed fragrant rice. Pass around soy sauce and sesame oil at the table. **SERVES 4**

... with Asian-style slaw

1 small (or ½ large) Chinese cabbage, shredded
2 sticks celery, shredded
2 carrots, peeled and shredded
3–4 small, crisp cucumbers, shredded
3–4 spring onions, thinly sliced lengthwise
mint leaves (Vietnamese, if available)
coriander leaves

DRESSING:
3 tablespoons fresh lime juice
3 tablespoons fish sauce
3 tablespoons peanut oil
2 tablespoons sugar
1 tablespoon rice vinegar
2 cloves garlic, crushed
2 fresh red chillies, chopped

Shred the pan-seared chicken fillets and mix with the cabbage, celery, carrot, cucumber and spring onion. Add a handful of mint and coriander leaves.

Mix the dressing ingredients. Pour over slaw and toss. **SERVES 4**

... with tomato & mushroom pasta sauce

1 x 400 g tin whole, peeled tomatoes in juice
1 clove garlic
handful of Italian parsley
salt and ground pepper
250 g white button mushrooms, sliced

Crush the tomatoes in their juice with garlic, parsley, salt and pepper. Turn into a non-stick pan and bring to a simmer. Add the mushrooms and allow to bubble for about 5 minutes, or until the mushrooms are just cooked and the tomatoes are reduced to a suitable saucy consistency. Stir in thinly sliced pan-seared chicken fillets and heat through.

Serve with 400 g just-cooked and drained spaghettini – reserve the pasta water. Mix the spaghettini with the sauce and about 70 g freshly grated Parmesan cheese. If necessary, loosen with a little of the reserved pasta water. Check seasoning and, if you like, add some more chopped parsley. Pass around Parmesan at the table. **SERVES 4**

… with verjuice, rocket & vegetable mash

Pour 1 cup verjuice into the pan you used to sear the chicken fillets. Allow to bubble and reduce until slightly syrupy. Set aside.

VEGETABLE MASH
500–750 g vegetable chunks (any mix of butternut, pumpkin, parsnip, carrot, celery root or turnip)
chicken stock
salt and ground pepper
crème fraîche (optional)

Cover vegetable chunks with chicken stock and simmer. Once tender, drain but set aside the liquid. Mash the cooked vegetables with a hand-held blender, adding the reserved cooking liquid if necessary. Add seasoning to taste and, if you like, a dollop of crème fraîche.

Serve the pan-seared chicken fillets with a generous mound of mash, moistened with the reduced verjuice and crowned with a handful of fresh rocket. **SERVES 4**

ONE TRADITIONAL ROAST,
Four other ways with turkey

No more difficult than roasting a chicken.
Prepare one for a festive occasion, and go
easy on other days with fresh free-range cuts.

Roast turkey with fresh herbs & white wine

1 free-range turkey (5–6 kg)
salt and ground pepper
melted butter or olive oil
some celery (chopped small) and fresh thyme, rosemary and oregano mix
2–3 onions
1–2 lemons
bay leaves
1 head garlic
2 cups chicken stock
2 cups dry white wine
watercress and cranberry sauce for serving

Remove any giblets and wash and dry the turkey well. Pull out any lumps of fat. Season all over and rub the skin with butter or olive oil. Stuff with lots of the celery and herb mix.

Add an onion, a lemon or two, a bay leaf and half the head of garlic. Bend wing tips under the body and tie the ends of the legs together.

Place in an oiled roasting pan. Roast, uncovered, at 200 °C for 30 minutes, or until lightly browned. Remove from oven. Reduce temperature to 180 °C. Add 1 or 2 sliced onions, a generous amount of chopped celery, the rest of the garlic, a few bay leaves and a mix of fresh herbs to the pan. Add the turkey neck, heart and cut-up gizzard. Pour over half the stock and wine. Cover with oiled greaseproof paper. Roast again, basting every 20 minutes or so, for 2 hours. Add more liquid if necessary. Remove paper and roast until golden brown and tender. Allow to rest for 15–20 minutes before carving.

To make gravy, stir the rest of the stock and wine into the roasting pan. Bring to the boil on the stove, stirring to loosen all the tasty brown bits. Boil, uncovered, for a few minutes. Check seasoning and strain into a gravy dish.

Garnish roast with lots of watercress. Serve with cranberry sauce and stove-top roast potatoes (boil until tender, skin and deep-fry in hot oil). **SERVES 10–12**

Pan-fried crumbed turkey

6 turkey schnitzels
salt and ground pepper
flour
2 free-range eggs, beaten with 2 tablespoons cream
plain home-made breadcrumbs (made from day-old bread)
sunflower oil
lemon wedges for serving

Pound the meat until thin. Season lightly. Coat meat all over in flour, shaking off the excess, then dip in egg mixture and finally coat with crumbs. (You can do this ahead of time and refrigerate to set the crumbs.)

Fry on both sides in hot oil until golden-brown and crisp. Serve with lemon wedges and a caesar salad made with roast diced potatoes instead of croutons (page 28). **SERVES 4–6**

Honey-soy glazed turkey buffalo wings

1 kg turkey wings
salt and ground pepper

FOR THE MARINADE, MIX TOGETHER:
½ cup peanut oil
¼ cup runny honey
2 tablespoons soy sauce
2 cloves garlic, crushed

Wash and dry the turkey wings. Season, then coat with the marinade.

Turn into a roasting pan lined with non-stick baking paper. Roast at 200 °C for about 1 hour, or until nicely browned, sticky and very tender.

Delicious with steamed tenderstem broccoli and jasmine rice. **SERVES 4**

Braised turkey cutlets with tomatoes on pasta

1 kg turkey cutlets
2 tablespoons olive oil
1 onion, thinly sliced
salt and ground pepper
2 cloves garlic, crushed
1 x 400 g tin whole, peeled tomatoes in juice, crushed
100 g sun-dried tomatoes

1 x 70 g tin tomato paste
¼ cup torn basil leaves
1 teaspoon dried oregano
1½ cups chicken stock
½ cup dry red wine
2 tablespoons balsamic vinegar
chunky pasta for serving; fresh basil and Parmesan cheese for garnishing

Wash and dry the turkey cutlets and cut into chunks. Heat the oil in a suitable casserole and brown the turkey in batches. Remove as ready and season. If necessary, add more oil.

Reduce the heat and add the onion with a little seasoning. Cook gently until soft. Stir in the garlic, tinned and sun-dried tomatoes, tomato paste and herbs. Return the turkey chunks to the pot. Pour in the stock and wine and bring to a simmer. Cover with a sheet of oiled greaseproof paper directly on the turkey, plus the lid. Bake at 160 °C in the oven for about 1 hour, or until the turkey is very tender. Stir in the balsamic vinegar and heat through. Check seasoning. **SERVES 6**

Roast rolled turkey breast & vegetables

1 rolled turkey breast (about 1.5 kg)
salt and ground pepper
olive oil
1.5 kg mix of vegetables (baby turnips, parsnips,
    carrots, cubed pumpkin and sweet potato)
handful of fresh thyme
1 cup chicken stock

Season and oil the turkey breast. Place in an oiled roasting pan.
Add the vegetables and flatten into a single layer. Tuck in fresh
thyme. Grind over some seasoning and drizzle with oil.

Bake at 190 °C for 45–60 minutes, or until nicely browned and
tender. Pour over the chicken stock, switch off the heat and leave
for 5–10 minutes. Remove the string, slice and serve with the pan
juices and vegetables. **SERVES 6**

ONE GREAT GRILL,
Dressed to thrill

Take a fresh fish cut, sear under and over,
then dress four ways.

BASIC GRILLED FISH

Choose a good, thick cut of fish, with skin if possible. Moisten with olive oil and season with sea salt and ground pepper. Don't marinate – simply sear, skin-side first, under a hot grill or over coals, until the skin is crisp and blistered. Then flip for a minute or two, flesh side to the heat. Cook until just done and still moist. It's a matter of minutes. Lift onto plates or a platter and spoon over one of the dressings on the following pages (quantities sufficient for 4–6 fish steaks).

KNOW YOUR FISH

The cardinal rule: the dish is as good as the fish. It has to be fresh to be delicious. Get your fishmonger to make the best choice for you.

HOW DO I KNOW IT'S FRESH?

- Sea-fresh fish does not smell.
- The flesh should be firm and springy when prodded.
- When buying a whole fish, check that the eyes are clear and protruding, the gills bright pinky-red and the body shiny.
- Buy fresh on the day of cooking. If bought the day before, lightly salt and refrigerate, then rinse and pat dry before using.
- On hot summer days, use an insulated container or cooler bag to transport the fish home.

SOME CHOICE CUTS

- **Thick firm-fleshed fillets:** are best for grilling and braaing.
- **Cape salmon:** one of the best.
- **Kabeljou:** a good bet too.
- **Yellowtail:** Just-cooked, still moist; a winner.
- **Tuna:** a real treat served rare.
- **Salmon:** Always pretty on the plate. See that it's done medium-rare.
- **Kingklip:** A tricky one. There's a point of perfection (hard to guess). If you pass it, you'll miss out on the texture that gives it its mass appeal.

Tahina & yoghurt dressing

250 g tahina dip
½ cup plain yoghurt
juice of 1 lemon
1 clove garlic, crushed
salt and ground pepper

Blend ingredients together and check seasoning. Pour over the just-cooked fish.

Serve with medium-sized couscous pasta or steamed baby potatoes and cos lettuce.

Tomato, mozzarella & anchovy dressing

4 firm, ripe tomatoes
1 ball soft mozzarella,
torn into shreds
4–6 anchovy fillets,
chopped
4 tablespoons olive oil
2 tablespoons balsamic
vinegar
handful of basil leaves
salt and ground pepper

Mix ingredients together and check seasoning. Pour over the just-cooked fish.

Serve with Parmesan-polenta mash and rocket.

Avocado, chilli & coriander dressing

1 ripe avocado
juice of 2 limes
1 green chilli, chopped
1 clove garlic, crushed
handful of coriander
leaves
1 cup buttermilk
salt and ground pepper

Mash the avocado pulp, then blend with the rest of the ingredients. If necessary, thin down with more buttermilk. Pour over the fish. Serve with sweet-potato fries and shredded, crisp lettuce.

Orange & sesame dressing

2 cups fresh orange juice
2 tablespoons honey
1 tablespoon soy sauce
1 chunk ginger, peeled and grated
1 clove garlic, crushed
2 tablespoons toasted sesame oil
salt and ground pepper
toasted sesame seeds for sprinkling

Simmer the orange juice, honey, soy sauce, ginger and garlic together for about 15 minutes, or until reduced and thickened. Stir in the sesame oil and season to taste. Pour over the just-cooked fish and sprinkle with sesame seeds.

Serve with Chinese noodles and steamed bok choy.

ONE GOOD STEAK,
Four great sauces

Take a steak to table …
plain and simple or sauced as you fancy.

BASIC PAN-GRILLED STEAK

About 250 g steak of your choice (rib-eye, rump, sirloin, fillet, T-bone) per person
salt and ground pepper
oil

Season the steaks, then oil the steaks, not the pan. Heat a suitable pan (ridged cast-iron, heavy non-stick or quality steel). Sear steak on both sides until it's a good colour.

Prod it to check if it's done: if soft, it's still rare; if springy to the touch, it's medium; if firm, it's (sadly) well done. If necessary, finish cooking the steaks at 180 °C for 5 minutes. Let it rest for a few minutes on a hot plate. Serve simply with good mustard or choose one of the sauces below or on the following pages. Add lots of watercress and some fried potatoes, or a split baked potato filled with butter.

Green peppercorn sauce

2 tablespoons soft green peppercorns (canned or bottled)
3 tablespoons brandy
½ cup cream
1 clove garlic, crushed

Rinse the peppercorns. Once the steaks are done, remove and pour the brandy into the pan. Allow to bubble away, then add the cream, lightly crushed peppercorns and garlic. Allow to reduce slightly. Check seasoning. (It may not need any, as the peppercorns tend to be salty.)

To serve, squash a thick medallion of fillet onto a large baked potato, then pour over the sauce. Great with watercress. **FOR 2 STEAKS**

Red wine & mushroom sauce

1–2 tablespoons butter

1 sprig fresh rosemary

250 g portabellini mushrooms, sliced

1 clove garlic, crushed

salt and ground pepper

½ cup dry red wine

½ cup beef stock

1 tablespoon balsamic vinegar

1 teaspoon honey

chopped Italian parsley

Heat the butter with the rosemary, add the mushrooms and garlic and briskly stir-fry for a minute or two until just cooked. Season lightly, remove from the pan and set aside.

Pour the wine, stock, vinegar and honey into the pan and allow to reduce. Return the cooked steaks, mushrooms and any juices to the pan and heat through. Check seasoning. Sprinkle with parsley to serve. **FOR 2–4 STEAKS**

Chimichurri

This Argentinian sauce, which tends to vary from home to home, is poured over grilled meat as it comes off the fire, but is often also used as a marinade. This version comes from one of my best-loved cookbooks, The Zuni Cafe Cookbook *by Judy Rogers (Norton & Co).*

1 red jalapeño chilli
2 teaspoons fresh oregano leaves
2 teaspoons fresh thyme leaves
1 teaspoon fresh rosemary leaves
about 1 cup good olive oil
1 tablespoon sweet paprika
1 tablespoon chopped Italian parsley
1–2 teaspoons finely chopped garlic
2 bay leaves, crumbled
2 tablespoons red wine vinegar
about ½ teaspoon salt
ground pepper

Grill the chilli under a hot grill or over the flame of a gas burner or open fire. Turn it over with tongs until freckled with black, about a minute. Allow to cool, then halve, seed and finely chop, not leaving out the tasty black blisters.

Bruise the oregano, thyme and rosemary in a mortar. Warm the olive oil in a small saucepan until hot to the touch. Remove from the heat and stir in the herbs, chopped chilli and remaining ingredients. (If you're making this sauce more than a few hours in advance, leave out the parsley and add nearer to serving time.) Check seasoning. Leave to infuse for at least 1 hour at room temperature. Spoon over the just-cooked, out-of-the-pan steaks. **FOR 4–6 STEAKS**

Tomato & onion sauce

This sauce can be made ahead and reheated before serving with the steaks.

1 onion, chopped
2 tablespoons olive oil
1 x 400 g tin whole, peeled tomatoes in juice
1 clove garlic, crushed
1 teaspoon paprika
1 teaspoon Worcestershire sauce
1 tablespoon chopped parsley
½ teaspoon dried oregano
salt and ground pepper
½ cup beef stock (optional)

Gently soften the onion in the oil. Blend the tomatoes with the juice in the tin and add to the pan. Stir in the garlic, paprika, Worcestershire sauce, parsley, oregano and a little seasoning. Simmer together, fairly briskly, for about 10 minutes, stirring often until reduced and thickened. If it gets too thick, thin down with stock. Check seasoning.

Good with steamed green beans and crusty pan-fried potatoes. **FOR 4 STEAKS**

ONE ROAST LAMB,
Four easy ways to flavour

Flattened for fast roasting, a free-range Karoo leg of lamb makes an impressive week-night dinner for friends.

ROAST BUTTERFLY LAMB

1 deboned, butterflied leg of lamb (1–1.5 kg)
salt and ground pepper
olive oil
1 head of garlic, halved
3–4 carrots, scraped and split
3–4 sticks celery
3–4 leeks, split
a handful of fresh herbs (a mix of rosemary, thyme and oregano)
½ cup dry red wine
1 cup beef or chicken stock

Remove any excess fat from the lamb. Season with salt and pepper and moisten with olive oil. Oil a suitably sized roasting pan and arrange the vegetables and herbs to form a 'rack' for the lamb. Place the lamb on top of the vegetables and roast at 190 °C for 30 minutes.

Pour over the wine and stock and roast for a further 15 minutes until nicely browned but still fairly rare inside. Remove the lamb, cover and rest while reducing the pan liquids on top of the stove. Season to taste, then strain into a heated gravy boat.

Garnish liberally with watercress.

ON THE SIDE: Roast potatoes. Use halved medium ones, lightly oiled and seasoned, roasted at the same time as the lamb. **SERVES 6**

... French country style

Follow the basic recipe, omitting the vegetable and herb rack and substituting the following ingredients:

3 x 410 g tins butter beans
200 g ready-to-use tomato pasta sauce
fresh rosemary
3–4 cloves garlic, crushed
¼ cup red wine
½ cup chicken or beef stock

Add the drained butter beans and tomato pasta sauce to the oiled roasting pan. Add lots of rosemary and mix in the garlic. Prepare and roast the lamb as directed on page 89. After about 30 minutes, pour over red wine and stock – there's no need to reduce on top of the stove.

ON THE SIDE: A mix of bitter greens – rocket, chicory or endive, small spinach leaves – tossed in olive oil and red wine vinegar.

... Italian style

Follow the basic recipe, omitting the vegetable and herb rack and substituting the following ingredients:

1 kg peeled, diced pumpkin
fresh sage leaves
2–3 cloves garlic, crushed
salt and ground pepper
olive oil
1 cup chicken stock
½ cup dry white wine

Arrange a bed of pumpkin in the oiled roasting pan. Tuck in sage leaves and add crushed garlic. Season and moisten with olive oil. Roast pumpkin at 190 °C for 30 minutes, or until tender.

Place the prepared lamb on top of the roasted pumpkin. Roast for 30 minutes. Pour over the stock and wine, and roast for a further 15 minutes.

ON THE SIDE: Cooked pasta tossed in good olive oil and a generous sprinkling of grated Parmesan, seasoned to taste.

... Thai style

Follow the basic recipe, omitting the vegetable and herb rack and substituting the following ingredients:

peanut oil
handful or two of spring onions
handful or two of lemon grass
1 cup chicken stock
2–3 tablespoons Thai red curry paste
1 x 400 g tin coconut milk
1 tablespoon fish sauce
2–3 teaspoons brown or palm sugar
1 fresh lime
handful of chopped coriander leaves

ON THE SIDE: Steamed fragrant rice and wilted Asian greens (bok choy, Chinese cabbage, tatsoi, etc.).

Moisten lamb with peanut oil. Place lamb on a bed of spring onions and lemon grass, pour over chicken stock and roast as directed (page 89). Once ready, remove the lamb, cover and rest. Pour off and reserve pan juices. On the stove, stir curry paste into roasting pan along with 2–3 tablespoons coconut milk. Once hot, stir in rest of coconut milk, ½ cup of reserved pan juices, fish sauce and sugar. Whisk and cook until slightly reduced. Add a squeeze of lime juice. Check sweet-sour balance – adjust if necessary. Stir in coriander.

... Greek style

Follow the basic recipe, omitting the vegetable and herb rack and substituting the following ingredients:

1 kg cooked potatoes, sliced
salt and ground pepper
3–4 cloves garlic, crushed
dried oregano
1 cup chicken stock
juice of 2 lemons

Arrange a bed of potatoes in the oiled roasting pan. Add seasoning, garlic and a sprinkling of oregano, and pour over stock. Place the prepared lamb on top and pour over the strained lemon juice. After roasting, garnish with wild rocket.

ON THE SIDE: Steamed green beans.

ONE EASY METHOD,
Four great casseroles

Get to grips with the basics,
then show off an impressive array of variation.

BASIC BEEF CASSEROLE

1 kg deboned beef shin, cut up
2–3 tablespoons oil
1 onion, chopped
12 sticks celery, chopped
12 carrots, chopped
1 fat clove garlic, crushed
1 cup dry red wine
2–3 cups beef stock
500 g peeled baby onions
a few sprigs rosemary

Pat the beef dry, then brown in batches in hot oil in a heavy casserole dish. Set meat aside.

Reduce the heat and, if necessary, pour in a little more oil. Stir in the onion, celery and carrots with a little salt and cook gently until softened. Stir in the garlic. Return the browned meat and any juices to the casserole dish. Pour in the wine and enough stock to just cover the browned meat. Bring to a bubble, and add the baby onions and rosemary. Place a piece of oiled, greaseproof paper directly on the surface. Place in the oven, heated to 160 °C, for 1½ –2 hours, or until fork-tender.

To finish, if you like, fry 250 g small, open brown mushrooms in hot butter and use to top each serving. Serve with buttery mashed potatoes, garnished with chopped Italian parsley. **SERVES 6**

Chicken casserole

Follow the basic beef casserole recipe (page 97), substituting the following ingredients:

8 chicken thighs (or a mix of thighs and drumsticks)
   instead of beef
1 cup dry white wine instead of red
2 cups chicken stock instead of beef stock
750 g mix of baby veg (carrots, parsnips, turnips, etc.)
   instead of baby onions
generous sprigs of thyme instead of rosemary

Bake in the oven for 45–60 minutes. Serve with short pasta.

Pork casserole

Follow the basic beef casserole recipe (page 97), substituting the following ingredients:

1 kg deboned pork neck, cubed, instead of beef
1 cup dry white wine instead of red
1 cup chicken stock instead of beef stock

ADD TO THE LIQUID INGREDIENTS:
1 x 400 g tin whole, peeled tomatoes in juice, crushed
juice and rind of 1 orange
1 fresh red chilli, split, instead of rosemary

Bake in the oven for 1–1½ hours. Serve with white or brown rice.

Lamb casserole

Follow the basic beef casserole recipe (page 97), substituting the following ingredients:

1.5 kg lamb knuckles instead of beef
500 g peeled, cubed sweet potato instead
  of baby onions
a few sprigs fresh oregano instead of
  rosemary
250 g baby spinach leaves

Bake for 1½–2 hours. Remove the casserole
from the oven and stir the spinach leaves
into the hot liquid until wilted. Serve with
soft polenta.

HOT TIPS FOR COOL CASSEROLES

- Invest in a good casserole dish – Le Creuset is excellent.
- If you don't have a stove-top casserole dish, start with a saucepan on top of the stove. Once the liquid is added, stir to loosen all the valuable sticky bits, then turn into an oiled baking dish and cover well.
- Allow meat to brown without stirring. If you try to turn the meat too soon, it will be difficult as the meat will stick to the pan. Once sealed, it'll release from the pan and can be easily turned. Season each batch of meat as it's browned.
- Gelatinous cuts like shin, knuckle and neck respond well to slow cooking.
- To peel baby onions, pour boiling water over them, cut off the ends, then slip off the skins.
- If there seems to be too much liquid, remove the cooked meat and vegetables with a slotted spoon and keep warm. Reduce the liquid by boiling it on top of the stove until slightly syrupy. This will intensify the flavour too.
- To remove any fat, chill the cooled casserole overnight, then spoon off the layer of fat before reheating. If serving straight after cooking, blot fat with paper towels.
- To add extra flavour:
  - to your chicken or beef casserole, add gremolata: chopped parsley with lemon rind, garlic and a few anchovies.
  - to your pork or lamb casserole, add coriander pesto: pounded coriander leaves, green chilli, garlic and a little olive oil.

MARVELLOUS MINCE,
Five versatile ways

Take a basic mix of tasty mince and make it fancy or keep it classic.

BASIC BEEF MINCE

1 large onion, chopped
2 tablespoons sunflower oil
12 fat cloves garlic, crushed
500 g lean beef mince (organic if available)
1 extra-large free-range egg
1 thick slice bread, white or wholewheat, soaked in water or stock
2 tablespoons chopped parsley
salt and ground pepper

First soften the onion in heated oil with a pinch of salt. Stir in the garlic, and mix with the mince. Remove from heat.

Beat the egg and mix with the squeezed, soaked bread and parsley. Add this to the mince and onion mixture, and knead well together. Season to taste.

Hamburgers

Shape the mince mixture into 4 large patties. Slide under a hot grill until well browned on both sides and slightly pink inside. (Or dust with flour and pan-fry in shallow oil over medium heat.) Split 4 large, round hamburger buns and spread with butter or mayonnaise and mustard. Sandwich with butter lettuce, sliced tomatoes, sliced sweet onion and a hot hamburger patty. Pass the tomato sauce/ketchup or hot chilli jam. **SERVES 4**

Roasted burgers
& potatoes

4 unpeeled potatoes
olive oil
salt and ground pepper

BBQ SAUCE:
½ cup beer
½ cup tomato sauce/ketchup
2 tablespoons soft brown sugar
2 tablespoons Worcestershire sauce
salt and ground pepper

Arrange 4 large hamburger patties on a large, oiled baking tray.
Put thinly sliced, unpeeled potatoes in a single layer on another
oiled baking tray. (If you like, line the baking trays with non-stick
baking paper.) Drizzle with olive oil and season to taste. Roast in
a fierce oven, 240 °C, for 20–30 minutes, or until the burgers are
browned and the potatoes are tender.

FOR THE BBQ SAUCE:
Simmer the ingredients together for 10 minutes.

Serve the burgers with BBQ sauce and a green salad. **SERVES 4**

Spicy Indian meatballs with coriander & egg

flour for dusting
2 tablespoons sunflower oil
1 x 400 g tin Indian-style tomatoes
2–3 hard-boiled eggs
handful of coriander
fresh lime juice
salt and ground pepper

Form the basic mince mixture (page 105) into 8–12 medium-sized patties. Dust with flour and brown in hot oil. Pour off the oil.

Pour tomatoes into the pan. Cover and simmer gently for about 20 minutes. Stir in quartered eggs and coriander leaves. Add a squeeze of lime juice and check seasoning.

Serve with basmati rice, sweet chutney and hot pickles on the side. **SERVES 4**

Meatballs in tomato sauce on orzo

flour for dusting
3–4 tablespoons sunflower oil
1 large onion, chopped
salt and ground pepper
1 clove garlic, crushed
1 box (500 g) crushed, strained tomatoes
1 cup beef or chicken stock
1 teaspoon dried oregano
80 g feta cheese

With wet hands, form the basic mince mixture (page 105) into tiny meatballs (about 40).

Dust with flour. Brown in batches in oil over medium heat in a wide pan, preferably non-stick. Set aside.

Pour off the oil and add 12 tablespoons fresh oil to the pan. Add the onion and cook gently with a pinch of salt until softened. Stir in the garlic, tomatoes, stock and oregano.

Return the meatballs to the pan, cover and simmer gently for about 15 minutes. Stir in crumbled feta and check seasoning.

Serve with hot, drained orzo (rice-shaped pasta) and garnish with fresh oregano. **SERVES 4**

Grilled kofta pitas

To the basic mince mixture (page 105), add:

1 teaspoon ground coriander
1 teaspoon ground cumin
½ teaspoon ground cinnamon
¼ teaspoon ground allspice

Shape the mince mixture into ovals, about 5 cm long (about 16 koftas), and thread onto slim bamboo sticks. Brown under a hot grill, about 5 minutes per side.

Serve in warm pitas, halved and stuffed with cos lettuce. Spoon over thick yoghurt mixed with chopped cucumber and fresh mint. **SERVES 4**

ROASTED WINTER VEG,
Five different dishes

Veggies, dressed up or down,
can easily hold their own at dinner.

BASIC ROASTED VEG

olive oil spray

1.5 kg peeled winter vegetable chunks (any mix of carrots, turnips, parsnips, swedes,
   pumpkin, butternut squash)

salt

fresh herbs (thyme, rosemary or oregano)

garlic cloves

Spray a large, shallow baking pan with olive oil. Arrange the chunks of vegetables in a single layer.
Season with salt and spray with olive oil.

Tuck in sprigs of herbs and some smashed garlic cloves. Roast at 230 °C, one shelf above the
middle of the oven, for 30–40 minutes, or until tender and starting to catch.

Serve straight out the oven with either crispy roasted butterflied chicken, rare roast beef or
roasted fish steaks. **SERVES 6–8**

... in a soup

Prepare a batch of roasted vegetables (page 115).

TO MAKE THE SOUP:
8 cups vegetable stock
3 tablespoons tomato paste

Heat the roasted vegetables with the stock. Stir in the tomato paste. Roughly purée with a hand-held blender so that the soup is thickened but has lots of texture.

Sprinkle with stir-fried slices of chorizo sausage, crumbled crispy bacon or cheesy croutons. **SERVES 6–8**

... with pasta

Prepare a batch of roasted vegetables (page 115).

TO MAKE THE PASTA SAUCE:
1 cup cream
1 clove garlic
handful of Italian parsley or basil leaves
salt and ground pepper
500 g drained, hot penne

Blend the cream, garlic and parsley or basil together. Heat and reduce slightly, then season to taste. Mix with the pasta and top with the veg.

Sprinkle generously with grated Parmesan cheese. **SERVES 6**

... as a salad

Serve a batch of roasted vegetables (page 115) with any mix of bitter salad leaves (spinach, chicory, radicchio, endive, rocket) and a dressing.

DRESSING:

3 tablespoons white wine vinegar

1 clove garlic, crushed

2 tablespoons chopped Italian parsley

1 teaspoon honey

1 teaspoon Dijon mustard

⅓ cup sunflower oil

⅓ cup olive oil

salt and ground pepper

Blend all the dressing ingredients together.

Toss the roasted vegetables with the dressing, then spoon over piles of washed salad leaves. SERVES 6–8

... in brown rice pilaf

Make this flavoured rice dish while the vegetables are roasting (page 115).

PILAF:

1 large onion, chopped

2 tablespoons sunflower oil

1 clove garlic, chopped

2 cups brown rice, uncooked

4 cups vegetable stock

salt and ground pepper

1–2 teaspoons dried oregano

250 g feta cheese

olive oil

Soften the onion in heated oil. Stir in the garlic and rice. Pour in the stock and a pinch of salt. Bring to a bubble, reduce the heat, cover and cook for 30 minutes, or until the liquid is absorbed and the rice is tender.

Turn into an oiled baking dish. Spoon over the roasted vegetables, sprinkle with oregano and crumble over the drained feta. Drizzle with olive oil and add a grinding of black pepper. Return to the hot oven until the feta starts to melt.

Serve with pasta-style tomato sauce. **SERVES 4–6**

STEAMED GREENS,
Four deliciously different ways

The heat is on, but not for long.
Steamed greens are quick to prepare.

BASIC STEAMED GREENS

500 g mix of trimmed greens (mangetout, sugar snap peas, asparagus tips, fine green beans)

Spread out the vegetables in a large steamer set in a wide pan. Steam over simmering water for about 10 minutes, or until tender-crisp. Serve with grilled chicken or salmon trout. **SERVES 6**

GET STEAMING

- Make sure that the water is simmering before you add the vegetables.
- Cover the pan tightly to prevent the steam from escaping.
- Expandable steel steamers are particularly useful as they fit any size saucepan.
- Tiered steamers (bamboo or metal) allow separation of ingredients. If they need different cooking times, each can be removed from the heat as soon as they are ready.
- A pasta pot, with its lift-out metal basket, can double up as a steamer.

... Chinese style

Steam 4 small soles or 400 g fish fillets and a handful of bean sprouts along with the greens.

DRESSING:
2 tablespoons rice vinegar
1 teaspoon honey
1 tablespoon soy sauce
4 tablespoons peanut oil
4 tablespoons sesame oil
1 red chilli, chopped
1 clove garlic, crushed
1 teaspoon crushed ginger

Mix the dressing ingredients together and pour over the fish, sprouts and greens. Check seasoning. Garnish with shredded spring onion and onion sprouts.

Serve with steamed jasmine rice. **SERVES 4**

… on the side with garlic-basil butter

FOR THE GARLIC-BASIL BUTTER:

60 g unsalted butter

2 cloves garlic, crushed

½ cup shredded basil leaves

squeeze of lemon juice

salt and ground pepper

Pound the ingredients together. Serve with rare pan-seared steaks (rib-eye or tuna). SERVES 4–6

... as a pasta topping

Toss drained, freshly cooked spaghettini with:

250 g mascarpone
1 tablespoon lemon juice
1–2 cloves garlic, crushed
salt and ground pepper

Mix this with half the steamed greens; spoon over the rest.

Add shavings of Parmesan cheese and moisten with olive oil.

SERVES 4

… as a salad

Toss steamed vegetables with a herb dressing.

DRESSING:

2 tablespoons lemon juice

1 clove garlic, crushed

salt and ground pepper

6 tablespoons olive oil

1 tablespoon chopped Italian parsley

1 tablespoon snipped chives

1 tablespoon chopped oregano

Whisk the dressing ingredients together. Spoon vegetables and dressing onto a mix of crisp and soft lettuce leaves. **SERVES 6**

ONE MERINGUE,
Four ways to impress

An all-time favourite,
meringues are miraculously easy to make.

THE MERINGUE RECIPE

6 extra-large free-range egg whites (at room temperature)
1 teaspoon cream of tartar
2 cups castor sugar
2 teaspoons white vinegar
2 teaspoons vanilla essence

Beat the egg whites with the cream of tartar until soft peaks form. Gradually add the castor sugar, beating well after each addition. Beat in the vinegar and vanilla essence and continue to beat the mixture until stiff and glossy.

Drop or pipe the mixture onto baking sheets lined with non-stick baking paper. Bake at 110 °C for 3 hours. Switch off the heat but leave to cool in the oven for a few hours, or overnight, until crisp.

Meringues with berry cream

Put out a pile of meringues and a bowl of thick cream swirled with crushed raspberries (fresh in season, frozen if not). Let guests help themselves.

Chocolate-nut meringue

meringue mix (page 135)
200 g dark chocolate
1 cup cream, whipped
jar of chocolate-hazelnut spread

Make four 20 cm meringue rounds. Bake at 120 °C for 3 hours, then cool in the switched-off oven.

Melt 200 g dark chocolate, then use a dessert spoon to drizzle chocolate over each layer of meringue. Lightly mix the whipped cream with the chocolate-hazelnut spread and use to sandwich the layers. **SERVES 8–10**

Lemon meringues

meringue mix (page 135)
1 tablespoon cornflour
lemon sauce (see below) or citrus sorbet

Heat the oven to 200 °C. Make the basic meringue mix but sift cornflour over the glossy meringue mixture and fold in gently.

Form 24 oval-shaped spoonfuls of meringue. Reduce oven temperature to 120 °C and place the meringues in the oven. Bake for 20 minutes.

Switch off the heat and leave for 1 hour before removing. Allow to cool. Serve the crisp-crusted, marshmallowy meringues with lemon sauce or a citrus sorbet.

LEMON SAUCE:
6 extra-large free-range egg yolks
⅓ cup castor sugar
juice and zest of 1 large lemon
½ cup cream, whipped
1–2 tablespoons Limoncello liqueur

Beat the egg yolks and sugar together, then beat in the lemon juice and grated rind. Cook gently together until thick, stirring constantly, taking care not to allow it to boil and curdle.

Remove from the stove and whisk until cool. Fold into the whipped cream and add liqueur to taste. **FOR 12 MERINGUES**

Sunshine pavlova

meringue mix (page 135)
selection of sliced yellow, golden or orange fruit (mango, papaya, sweet melon, pineapple,
    peaches, plums)
granadilla pulp (optional)

Make the meringue in the same way as for the lemon meringues (page 139). Spread a 23 cm circle
of meringue on non-stick baking paper. Using the back of a spoon, make a shallow depression in
the centre and build up the sides. Bake at 150 °C for about 30 minutes until risen and a pale
brown. Reduce the heat to 140 °C and bake for a further 45 minutes. Switch off the heat and leave
in the oven for a few hours. Take out and cool before removing from the paper.

   Fill the meringue base a few hours before serving. Pile with fruit of your choice, top with
granadilla pulp, and serve with vanilla or mango ice cream. SERVES 8–10

FLOP FIXER

Broken meringues? Mix the crumbled meringues with whipped cream, custard or ice cream and
crushed berries – fresh in season, otherwise frozen. (Defrost berries slowly in the fridge in a strainer.)

- It's easier to separate eggs that have been refrigerated, but allow egg whites to reach room
  temperature before whisking them.
- Use egg yolks for mayonnaise, sweet custards or savoury tarts.
- Don't make meringues when it's humid or there's moisture in the air.
- Crisp meringues keep well in airtight containers. Ones filled with ice cream or cream should
  be frozen to store.

ONE EASY BATTER,
Five fabulous cakes

A piece of cake!
Baking was never easier.

EASY YOGHURT CAKE

1 small tub (175 ml) plain yoghurt

USING THE SAME TUB AS A MEASURE, ADD:
1 tub sunflower oil
2 tubs sugar
3 tubs self-raising flour
pinch of salt
3 extra-large free-range eggs
1 teaspoon natural vanilla extract

Empty the tub of yoghurt into a large mixing bowl. Add the rest of the ingredients. Using an electric beater, beat well until smooth. Pour the batter into a cake tin, loaf or ring mould, coated with non-stick cooking spray.

Bake at 180 °C for about 45 minutes until springy to the touch or an inserted tester comes out clean. Leave for 5–10 minutes to cool slightly before removing from tin. Allow to cool completely on a cake rack. Dust with icing sugar before serving.

The cake will keep well in an airtight container.

Chocolate vermicelli squares

1 small tub (175 ml) chocolate-chip yoghurt

USING THE SAME TUB AS A MEASURE, ADD:
1 tub sunflower oil
2 tubs treacle sugar
2 tubs self-raising flour
¼ cup cocoa powder
pinch of salt
3 extra-large free-range eggs
1 teaspoon natural vanilla extract
100 g chocolate vermicelli

Bake in a deep, square cake tin (20 x 5 cm) for about 45 minutes. Glaze the cooled cake with 50 g dark chocolate melted with 2 tablespoons cream, and cut into squares to serve.

Vanilla
layer cake

Use vanilla yoghurt instead of plain yoghurt in the easy yoghurt cake recipe (page 143). Bake in two 20 cm cake tins for about 30 minutes. Sandwich and cover with vanilla icing (below).

VANILLA ICING:
250 g soft butter
500 g icing sugar
1 teaspoon natural vanilla extract

Whip the ingredients until the icing is light and fluffy.

Lemon loaf

Add the zest of 1 lemon to the easy yoghurt cake batter (page 143). Bake in a 23 cm loaf pan. Mix the juice of the lemon with 1 tablespoon sugar, and spoon this over the cake as soon as it comes out the oven.

Strawberry cream cake

Bake the easy yoghurt cake (page 143) in two 20 cm cake tins for about 30 minutes. Sandwich with sweetened whipped cream and strawberries, and dust the top with icing sugar. Or, for the sophisticated adult, a single layer topped with strawberries. The second layer can be simply iced for kids.

INDEX

First published in 2007 by Struik Publishers
(a division of New Holland Publishing (South Africa) (Pty) Ltd)
Cape Town * London * Sydney * Auckland
www.struik.co.za

Cornelis Struik House, 80 McKenzie Street, Cape Town 8001, South Africa
Garfield House, 86–88 Edgware Road, London W2 2EA, United Kingdom
Unit 1, 66 Gibbes Street, Chatswood, NSW 2067, Australia
218 Lake Road, Northcote, Auckland, New Zealand

New Holland Publishing is a member of Avusa Ltd

2 4 6 8 10 9 7 5 3

PUBLISHING MANAGER: Linda de Villiers
MANAGING EDITOR: Cecilia Barfield
EDITOR & INDEXER: Joy Clack
DESIGNER: Beverley Dodd
PHOTOGRAPHER: Craig Fraser
STYLIST: Phillippa Cheifitz
FOOD PREPARATION: Andrea Steer and Nici Beaumont,
Kirsty Ratcliffe (pages 64–71)
PROOFREADER: Carla Masson

Reproduction by Hirt and Carter Cape (Pty) Ltd
Printed and bound by Kyodo Printing Co (Singapore) Pte Ltd

ISBN 978 1 77007 207 7